Contents

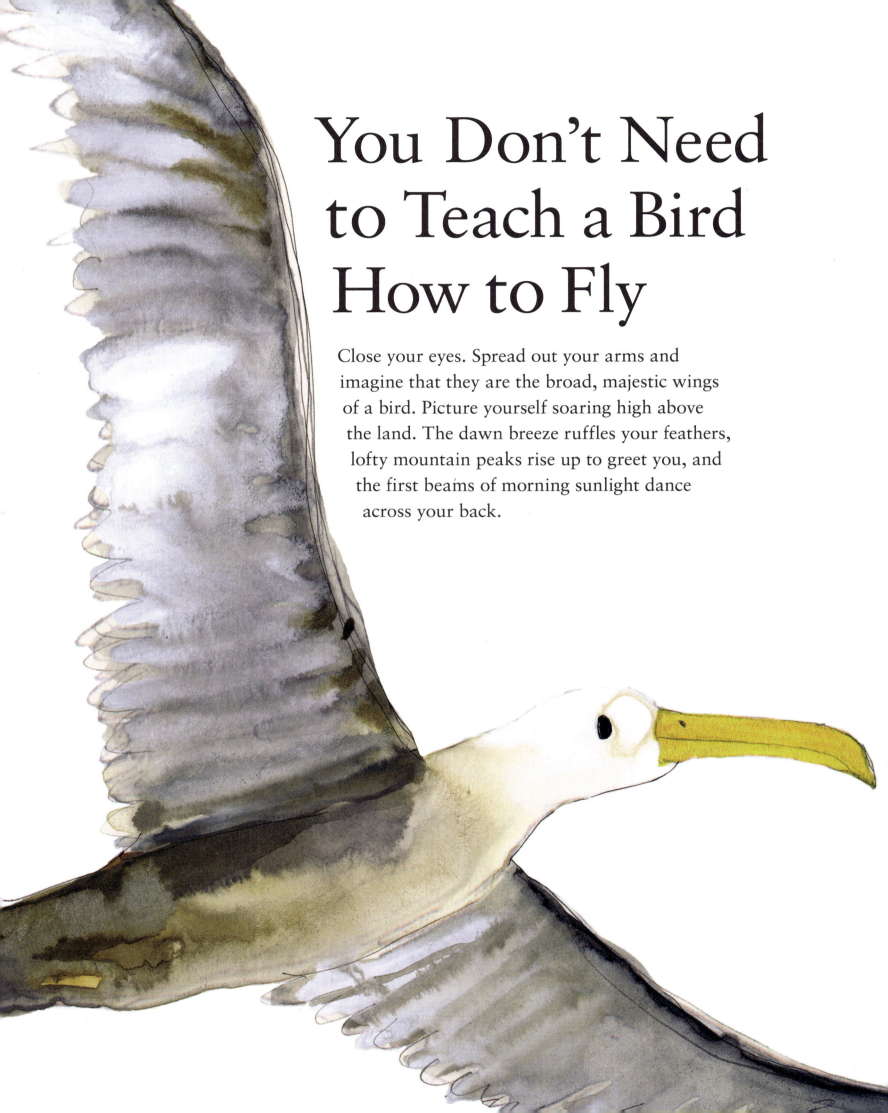

You Don't Need to Teach a Bird How to Fly

Close your eyes. Spread out your arms and imagine that they are the broad, majestic wings of a bird. Picture yourself soaring high above the land. The dawn breeze ruffles your feathers, lofty mountain peaks rise up to greet you, and the first beams of morning sunlight dance across your back.

You climb higher and higher, riding the golden sunrise. Your flight is effortless and beautiful. You were born for this.

You are a bird.

Many of us have dreamed about flying, but what would it really feel like to be a soaring eagle? Or an owl floating through night skies? Our five senses – sight, hearing, taste, smell and touch – are what we use to understand and recognise everything around us. Some birds' senses are similar to ours, but others are quite different. Humans and birds both use their eyes to see, but most birds have eyes on the sides of their heads, giving them two different views of the world at the very same time. Imagine that!

Bird behaviour is typically quite different to human behaviour. What would it be like to feel the urge to set off southwards in the autumn and northwards in the spring, like so many birds do every single year? Or imagine what it is like to fly across stormy oceans and splashing whales for thousands of miles and yet somehow know exactly where home is?

Of course, not all birds can fly. And there are countless other ways that birds are different from one another.

Picture a **squawking** *cockatoo, a paddling duck ... a tiny, fluttering jewel-green hummingbird ... or an* **enormous** *ostrich sprinting across the dusty desert.*

With their incredible versatility, birds have evolved their own special ways to survive in different habitats, from tropical rainforests to icy polar seas and wet, squidgy swamps.

All over the world, birds use their extraordinary and amazing skills – such as perching, preening, singing and nesting – to help them adapt and thrive. This book will share the survival secrets of some of the most astonishing animals on Earth.

Let's discover what it's like to be a bird ...

The beautiful female manakin does not look like the male. Her fine, olive-green feathers merge perfectly with the rainforest leaves.

Birds Can Dance

South and Central America

Deep in the rainforest, a band of nervous performers hop from leg to leg, each waiting to play their part. They are male red-capped manakins. Branches tremble and leaves rustle high up in the trees. From a branch above, a female red-capped manakin waits.

The male comes forward. This delicate little bird may be teeny-tiny in size, but when he puffs up his feathers and steps into the spotlight, all of the females pay attention.

It is the breeding season and the male red-capped manakin has a very important job to do. He needs to attract a partner to mate with. The bird turns his head to eye up the rest of the competition, showing off his magnificent scarlet plumes and sunshine yellow socks.

The performance begins. The male shuffles along the branch, fixing his gaze like a mechanical toy. Head down, tail up, he slides back and forwards along his perch. The funny clockwork dance is fascinating and some of the females flutter closer …

Then, the manakin is ready for his big finale. He jumps up and lands again on his perch, stunning the crowd with a noisy snapping sound.

BANG!

The bird makes the sound by rubbing his wings along his tail, three times. He does it so fast that it sounds like a gun going off! During the backwards shuffle he adds four more explosive BANGS! Bravo!

BANG! BANG! BANG! BANG!

Now, the females must judge the dance competition. One by one, each member of the audience will assess the quality of the dancers' sounds and movements before they choose the best performing male.

After mating, the female red-capped manakin finds the perfect spot to build a nest, ready for her chicks to hatch.

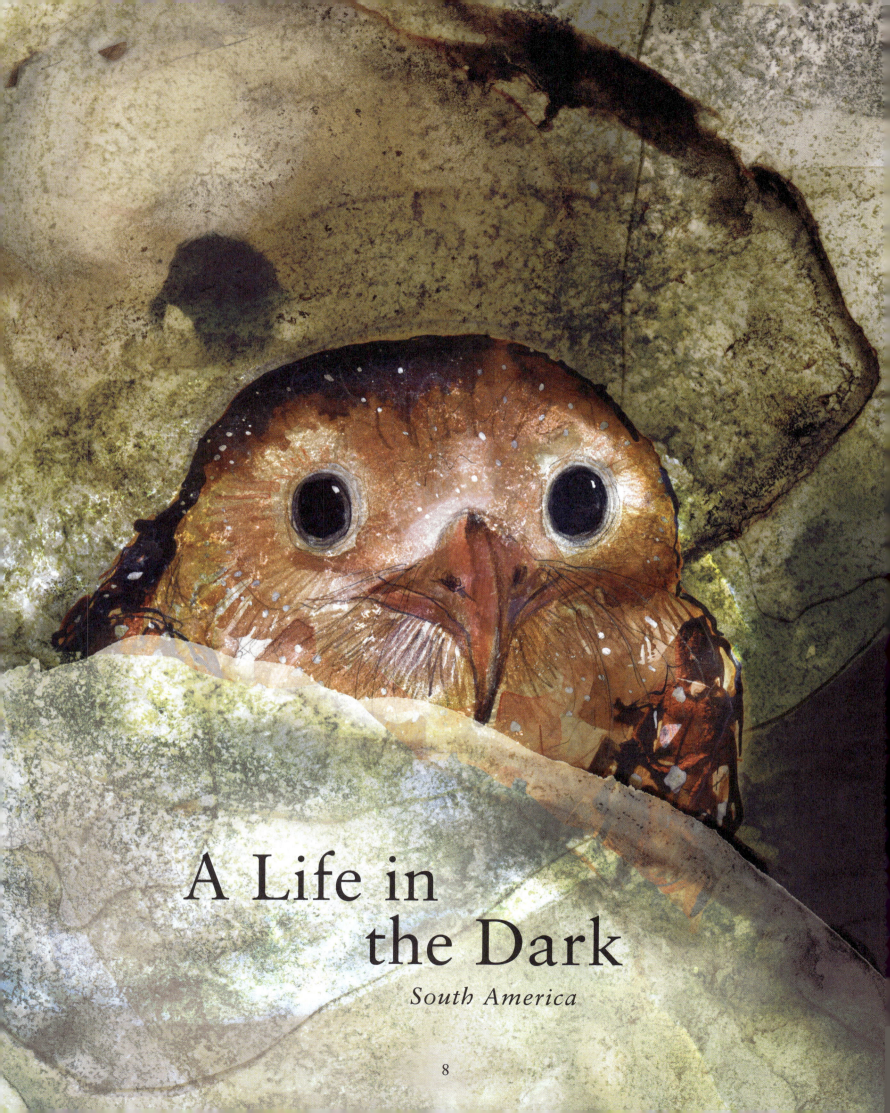

A Life in
the Dark

South America

*With a wingspan of almost a metre, the oilbird
has a long feathery tail, a hooked beak and
gorgeous, russet-red plumage that is decorated
with rows of tiny white hearts.*

A rustle, a shriek and
a click-click-click –
we are not alone in this cave!
Is a frightening monster hiding in
the darkness?

The curious oilbird roosts in the pitch-black caves
of South America, sometimes in colonies of up to 20,000
other oilbirds. Just like a bat, the oilbird uses a special
listening skill called echolocation to find its way safely back
to its perch.

During echolocation, the oilbird makes shrieking and clicking
sounds, then listens for the echoes bouncing off nearby objects. This
helps it to tell how far away the objects are so it won't bump into
them.

The oilbird is a vegetarian and its chicks are reared on oily fruit.
Eventually, the youngsters will grow into great featherballs of
fat – or oil – that's how the oilbird got its name!

Finding fruit in the dark can be a challenge, but oilbirds are experts.
These birds have very large, sensitive eyes – the most light-sensitive of any
animal species – which are perfect for peering into the gloom to look for
food.

Once it finds some fruit, the oilbird uses its broad wings to hover
alongside hanging fruit. The oilbird smells the fruit before it decides
which ones are ripe and ready to eat for supper.

King and Queen of the River

Europe and North America

As the sun slowly sets, a pair of mute swans glide majestically across the lake.

Side-by-side, they sail up and down the water patrolling their kingdom. They both know exactly where their territory starts and ends. They also know who their neighbouring swans are.

Swans have a rule: do not cross this line – enter at your peril!

The swans' territory is important because it contains all the food the pair need for themselves and a future family of cygnets. The birds do not want any other swans coming and helping themselves to this food.

Finally, they reach their nest, hidden amongst the bulrushes close to the bank. The location is carefully chosen – a huge, flat mound of dead reeds, grasses and waterweeds is an impressive construction. This is where the female swan will soon start to lay her eggs.

But good territories are hard to find, and sometimes another pair of swans will try to seize a stretch of river from its owners. When this happens, the resident male swan raises his wings and starts to hiss, swimming as fast as he can towards the intruders. He charges across the water with his head down, ready to peck.

There is a rush of flapping wings and splashing water as he becomes airborne.

PECK! PECK! PECK!

He is successful and the trespassers take flight. All is quiet on the river once more.

La la la la!

Choir Practice

Australia

It is early morning in Australia – a cool and shady hour before the yellow-white blaze of daytime. A flock of beady-eyed magpies fly down from their roosting trees and settle on the ground.

Five ... six ... seven ... eight ... more and more magpies appear.

The birds walk across the dry Australian countryside to an old fence post at the edge of a field. Standing in a circle around the post with their heads pointing towards the sky, the birds start to sing together, greeting the sunrise with a hauntingly beautiful, warbling song – they are a choir!

After ten minutes, the singing is over. As the sun rises in the sky, the choir breaks up and the birds go their separate ways for the day.

La la la la!

La la la la!

The Australian magpie is different to the Eurasian magpie ... It does not have a long tail, but it is slightly larger with a heavier beak. It is also more aggressive.

Unlike other magpies, Australian magpies live in groups rather than pairs. All members of the group work together to rear their young and defend their territory from anyone that comes into their home patch.

During their early morning song, the magpies come together to sing as a team – just like people in a choir, even if they cannot sing very well! Or like ... warriors of the past chanting together before going into battle ... or crowds at football matches singing before a big match.

Singing together feels good!

Perhaps the birds' early morning song helps them get ready for the day ahead.

La la la la!

La la la la!

La la la la!

The Ice and the Cradle

Antarctica and the Southern Ocean

The bitter wind howls and rages, for hour after hour. Dark sky reigns over land and sea. The emperor penguin looks down at the egg resting gently on his feet. He will wait as long as it takes …

Emperor penguins live in one of the most extreme environments on Earth – Antarctica. For their babies to survive in this harsh, frozen land, emperor penguins have to do something spectacular.

It begins with an egg.

After the female lays the egg, she passes it quickly onto her partner's feet. Then the male penguin uses a large, loose flap of skin on his lower belly to cover the egg – a bit like a pouch. On the inside of the flap there are no feathers at all – just bare pink skin that is rich with blood vessels. The blood carries the heat from the penguin's body to this skin, so the pouch acts as a hot water bottle that keeps the egg warm.

Once she is certain that the male penguin has got the egg comfy and tucked in place, the female goes off to sea so she can feed.

The new father is left all alone for two full months. During this time, and with no chance of eating, the hungry male will lose about half his weight, burning up all the fat he has stored in his body.

14

Emperor penguins are the largest species of penguin. They can grow to around 115 centimetres.

Just as the egg is ready to hatch, the mother penguin returns from the sea. Now rather plump, she is carrying a stomach full of squid and fish ready to give to the new arrival.

How does the mother know exactly when to come back?

The female penguin has a biological clock inside her brain that tells her when the egg is about to hatch.

As soon as the female has taken the chick from her partner and positioned it safely on her own feet, the male sets off for the sea to find food for himself and to recover from his long bout of babysitting.

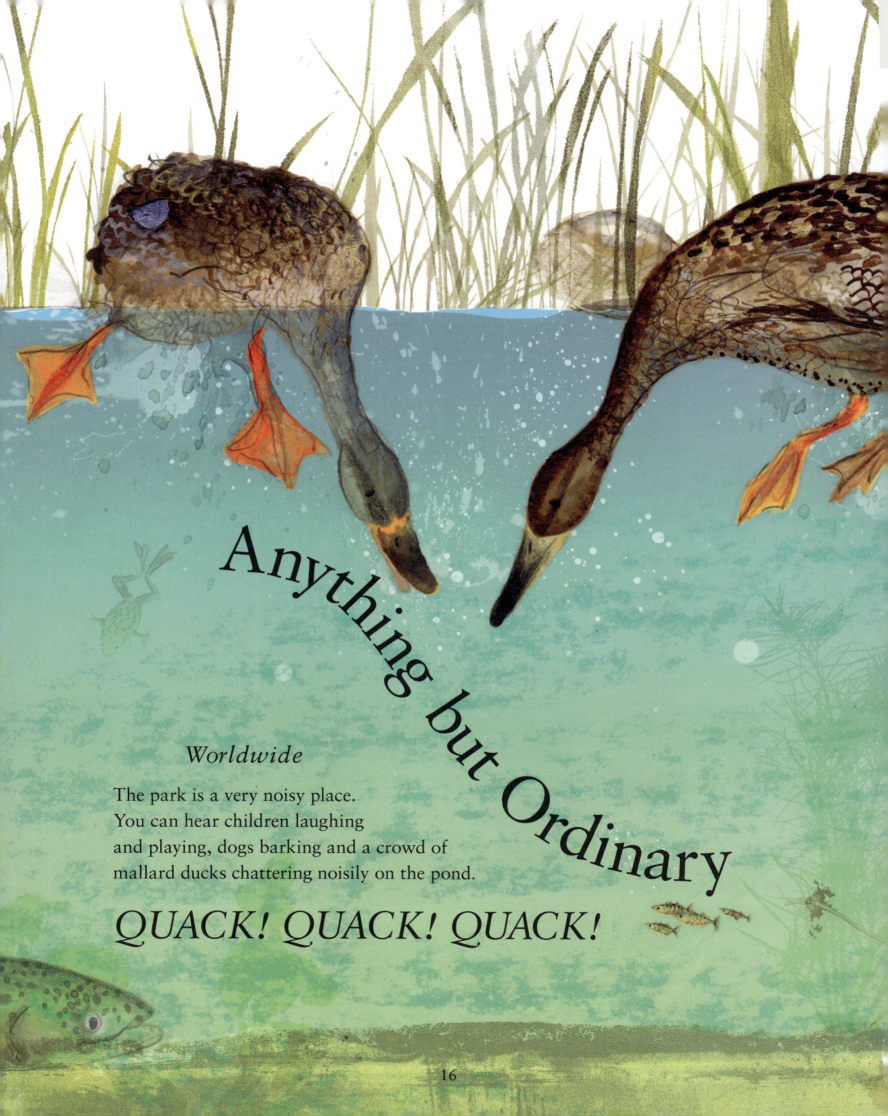

Anything but Ordinary

Worldwide

The park is a very noisy place.
You can hear children laughing
and playing, dogs barking and a crowd of
mallard ducks chattering noisily on the pond.

QUACK! QUACK! QUACK!

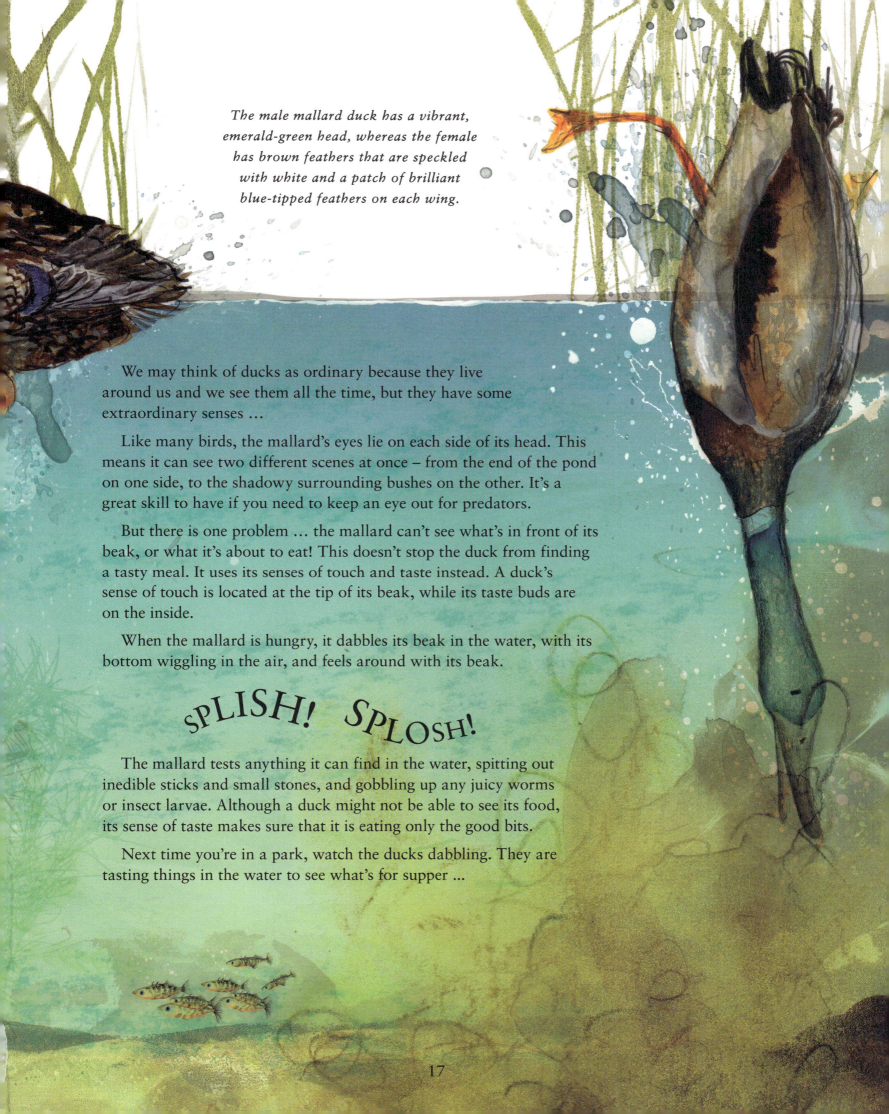

The male mallard duck has a vibrant, emerald-green head, whereas the female has brown feathers that are speckled with white and a patch of brilliant blue-tipped feathers on each wing.

We may think of ducks as ordinary because they live around us and we see them all the time, but they have some extraordinary senses …

Like many birds, the mallard's eyes lie on each side of its head. This means it can see two different scenes at once – from the end of the pond on one side, to the shadowy surrounding bushes on the other. It's a great skill to have if you need to keep an eye out for predators.

But there is one problem … the mallard can't see what's in front of its beak, or what it's about to eat! This doesn't stop the duck from finding a tasty meal. It uses its senses of touch and taste instead. A duck's sense of touch is located at the tip of its beak, while its taste buds are on the inside.

When the mallard is hungry, it dabbles its beak in the water, with its bottom wiggling in the air, and feels around with its beak.

SPLISH! SPLOSH!

The mallard tests anything it can find in the water, spitting out inedible sticks and small stones, and gobbling up any juicy worms or insect larvae. Although a duck might not be able to see its food, its sense of taste makes sure that it is eating only the good bits.

Next time you're in a park, watch the ducks dabbling. They are tasting things in the water to see what's for supper …

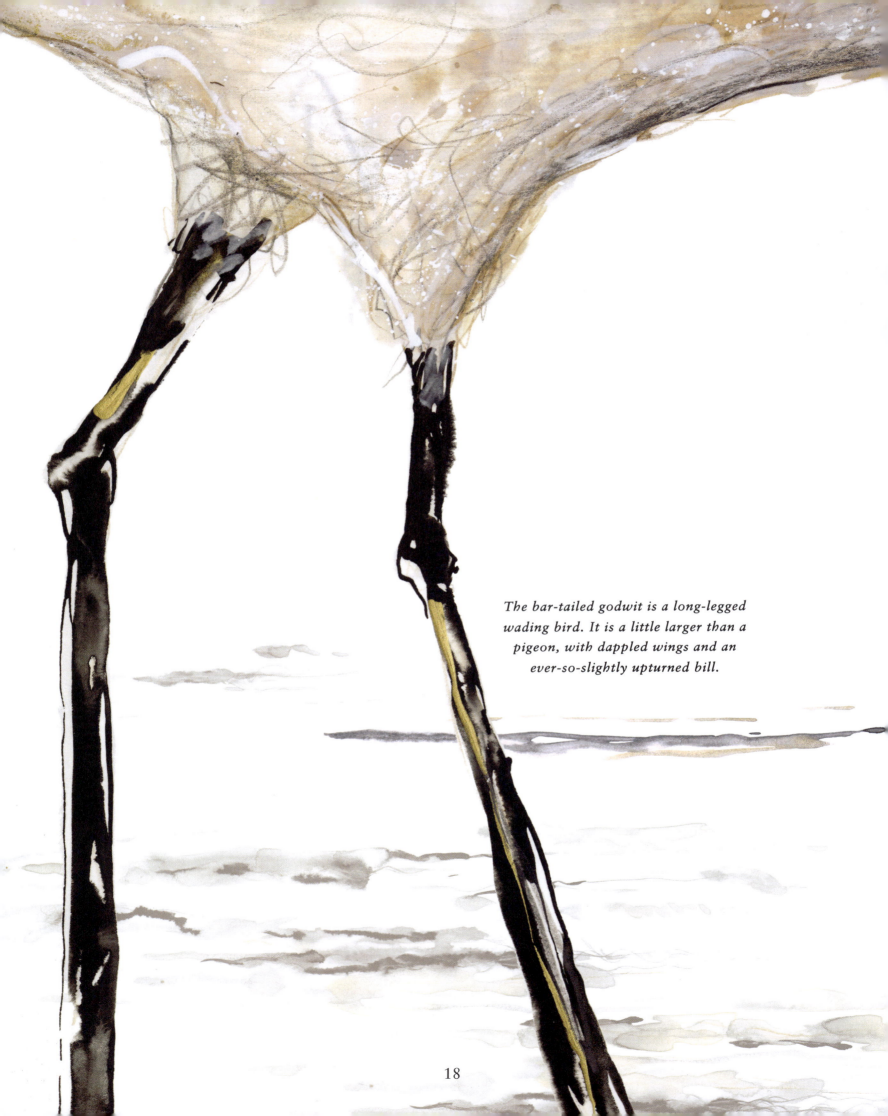

The bar-tailed godwit is a long-legged wading bird. It is a little larger than a pigeon, with dappled wings and an ever-so-slightly upturned bill.

Across the Sea

*Summers in Alaska, and winters
in New Zealand*

The ocean is still, spread out below like a roll of crumpled blue silk. The bar-tailed godwit flaps hard on the breeze, its wings cresting on currents of warm air. Winter fades away behind and the golden arms of summer stretch out to greet this old, familiar friend.

Like us, birds need food to survive. When we run out of supplies we can go to the shops. Birds cannot do this, so what do they do when their food runs out? Migrating birds like the godwit migrate between a summer and winter home – it's the only way to make sure that they have enough food throughout the year.

The godwit spends its summer in Alaska, North America. The bird breeds on the flat, treeless tundra, feeding on the many insects that live there. Then, at the end of the breeding season, the godwit says farewell and sets off for its winter home.

There are no warm, safe places to live just around the corner from Alaska, so every year the godwit makes an epic journey to New Zealand, thousands of miles away. The route is almost entirely over the sea. It would take us almost an entire day to fly that far in a comfy jet aeroplane. There is nowhere for a godwit to take a rest during its flight though. The bird must keep going – flying for eight days without stopping!

How does the godwit find its way? There are no landmarks on the ocean. Luckily, the bird has a biological sat nav inside its head that tells it where to go. It is one of nature's many marvels.

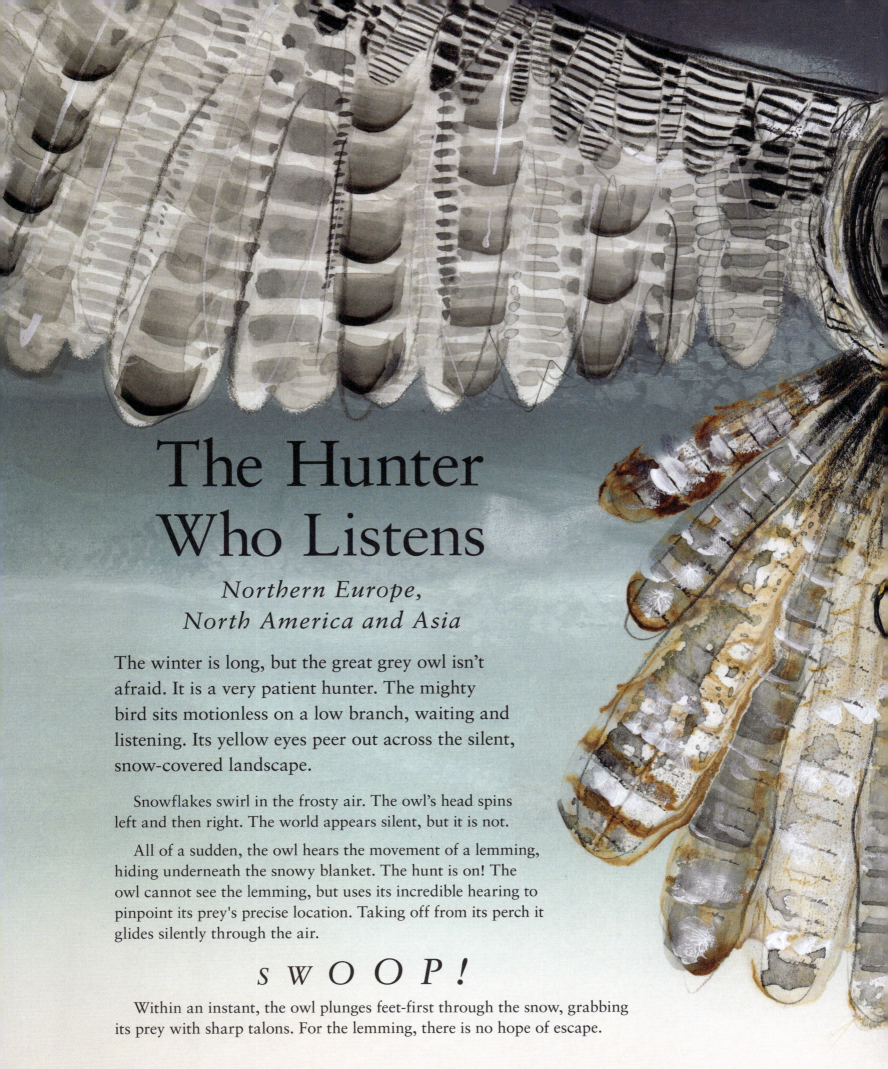

The Hunter Who Listens

*Northern Europe,
North America and Asia*

The winter is long, but the great grey owl isn't afraid. It is a very patient hunter. The mighty bird sits motionless on a low branch, waiting and listening. Its yellow eyes peer out across the silent, snow-covered landscape.

Snowflakes swirl in the frosty air. The owl's head spins left and then right. The world appears silent, but it is not.

All of a sudden, the owl hears the movement of a lemming, hiding underneath the snowy blanket. The hunt is on! The owl cannot see the lemming, but uses its incredible hearing to pinpoint its prey's precise location. Taking off from its perch it glides silently through the air.

s w O O P !

Within an instant, the owl plunges feet-first through the snow, grabbing its prey with sharp talons. For the lemming, there is no hope of escape.

For much of the year, the great grey owl's territory is covered in snow. Lemmings survive by burrowing in the grass beneath the carpet of white. The only way that the owl can work out where the lemmings are is to listen out for them moving around underneath the surface.

Humans would struggle to hear a lemming under the snow, let alone know where it was hiding, but the great grey owl is born for this job!

Beneath its head feathers it has two very large ears, which sound is funnelled towards. The owl's ear openings are located at different heights, so that sounds reach each one at very slightly different times, which helps the owl to pinpoint the source of the sound. The feathers of the owl's face form a wide circle around the eyes, funnelling sounds back towards the ears.

When it comes to listening, no one can outwit the great grey owl.

The great grey owl is the largest of all owls. Living in the forests of the far north, this master predator thrives in very harsh conditions.

Birds Around a Honey Pot

Africa

The honeyguide flits from perch to perch – it has exciting news to share! Up ahead, a man chops wood in the village. The dowdy little bird makes a whistle and, suddenly, the man puts down his axe. His face lights up and he follows the honeyguide into the shady forest …

In some parts of Africa, the honeyguide has a very special relationship with the local people. It helps them to find wild bees' nests so they can collect the sweet honey inside.

Wild bees usually nest inside a hollow tree or in a hole in the ground, building their honeycombs from wax that they make themselves.

Sniff the air. Imagine that you can smell bees' wax inside a nest over more than a kilometre away … that's exactly what the honeyguide can do!

The insides of the honeyguide's nostrils at the base of its beak are extremely sensitive to the scent of honey wax.

When a honeyguide gets a whiff of bees' wax on the air, it follows the smell until it finds the bees' nest. It remembers where the nest is, then it flies off to find someone.

As soon as the bird comes across a person, the honeyguide makes a special call that seems to say,

'Follow me, I'll take you to some yummy honeycomb!'

The local people love honey, so they follow the bird all the way to the nest and then take out the honeycomb – but they are always careful to thank the honeyguide by leaving a piece of honeycomb for it to eat.

This unlikely partnership depends on the people rewarding the honeyguide, but also on the bird's remarkable sense of smell.

Falling from the Skies
Worldwide

Flying very high, the peregrine falcon scans the land far below with sharp, beady eyes. It fixes a pigeon within its sights and then closes its wings. The drop is effortless and deadly – the horizon soon disappears as the falcon falls through the air at dizzying speed.

WHOOSH!

The peregrine falcon is the fastest bird in the sky. It is rapid in ordinary flight, but when it dives down towards its prey, the bird can reach record-breaking speeds. Pigeons are fast-fliers too, so to catch enough food to survive, the peregrine has to be even faster.

Spotting pigeons from a distance requires excellent eyesight. Most of us think of our own eyesight as good, but the peregrine's vision is far better, and it can see things much further away than we can.

Peregrines have better sight than us because of the way that their eyes are designed. The words on this page are clear to you because they are in line with a special area on the inside surface of your eye called the 'fovea'. This is a tiny place on the back of the eye where everything that you see is brightest and sharpest.

Move your head very slightly to one side and, without moving your eyes back to the letters, you'll see that the words on this page are less clear. It is only when we look directly at something that the image sits on the fovea so that we can see it clearly.

We have one fovea in each eye, but some birds, including the peregrine, have two – one for distance and one for close-up. The distance fovea is used for spotting prey, like pigeons, from far away – a bit like a telephoto lens.

No wonder the peregrine is such a super zoomer!

The peregrine falcon is able to dive or 'stoop' at over 300 kilometres (186 miles per hour).

The Fox and the Bird

*Southern Europe, but introduced
to the UK and New Zealand*

You are a baby chick – the last of ten brothers and sisters to
peck your way out of an egg. Now it is your turn to emerge,
a stripy ball of fluff bobbing and blinking up at the daylight.
Even though you are just a few hours old, you are already able
to run! Your mother – a partridge – is there to lead the way.

The most important thing for the mother is to keep her little ones safe
long enough to become grown-up partridges.

She is always on the lookout. Danger lurks around every corner ...

A fox, a stoat or a hawk would gobble up any baby partridge that
dares to stray across its path.

In the distance, the mother partridge sees a crow flying over the edge
of the field - this signals that there is a predator nearby. The partridge
must act quickly to protect her family. Quickly, she calls softly to her
chicks and gathers them around her. Then she leads the brood under the
hedge and out of sight.

As the partridge family start to come out of the other side, a fox
looms up from the shadows! Oh no, the fox has spied the mother!
But it has not seen the chicks in the long grass.

There is no time for the mother partridge to lead her babies away. She has to try something else. She pretends to have a broken wing, flopping along the track with one wing hanging by her side.

It looks like she cannot fly.

The fox, hoping for an easy meal, chases the partridge while she runs and flops, faster and faster, further and further away from her hidden chicks. Then, just as the fox pounces, the clever mother partridge bursts into the air and flies off!

She has tricked the fox by luring it so far away from her chicks that there's no chance he will find them now. The disappointed fox skulks away. When the mother partridge senses that it is safe, she runs back to find her family, calling the little birds out of their hiding place, ready to continue their journey.

Female red-legged partridges are unusual because they will often build two nests and lay eggs in each. The male and female each take care of a set of chicks and raise them independently.

27

Sledging for Beginners

Northern Hemisphere

One heavy winter snowfall, a soft, thick, white blanket covers the hills, trees and rooftops. Perched high on a sloping hillside is a group of stark, black ravens. One brave bird steps forward and peers over the edge. One … two … three … he leaps off, sliding down on his front.

WHEEEEEEEEE!

Completely covered in feathers and with a hefty bill, the plucky raven rolls over a few times before steadying himself once more. Despite being able to fly, this raven trudges back up to the top on foot and joins the rest of the flock, who are waiting for their turn to slide. They are just doing this for fun!

Ravens are playful birds, but they are incredibly intelligent too.

28

It can be difficult for many birds to find food in the winter, but the crafty raven knows what to do. He seeks out a rubbish bin left by humans. He can smell that there is some leftover food inside. With a sharp thrust of his beak, the lid flips up. The rest of the flock join him for the feast.

Ravens living in captivity have been known to solve man-made puzzles that would baffle a dog or a squirrel or indeed almost any other bird. Some captive ravens can even count ...

One ... two ... three ... four ... five.

You could play a game with a raven, but be warned: ravens are thought to be one of the cleverest species of bird, so they might be able to outsmart you!

Ravens are sociable birds and will often spend their whole life with the same partner. They can live for around thirteen years – that's a long time to spend together! In winter, pairs of ravens join others to roost in large flocks.

The sungrebe looks like a little duck. It can
swim, run and clamber through reeds and
low-hanging branches.

Ready for Take-off

Central and South America

The river sparkles in the tropical afternoon light. Branches sway and dance, dipping their tips in the gently flowing water. A reed snaps. Insects buzz.

No one has noticed the secretive little bird hiding in the undergrowth ...

The sungrebe paddles through the shallows. This is where it spends most of its time, swimming and diving in slow-moving, freshwater streams. Its nest is tucked into the side of the riverbank, out of sight.

In her nest, the mother sungrebe lays just two eggs, and – unlike most other bird species – when they hatch it is the father who looks after the chicks. He performs his duties almost entirely on his own.

The chicks can swim soon after they hatch, but if danger threatens, the father has a very unusual way of keeping his two babies out of trouble ...

Tucked away under each of his wings is a very special pouch. If the male sungrebe gets anxious, the bird simply hides a chick in each of the pouches and then swiftly flies off with them, whisking the family out of harm's way.

Before he makes his escape, the sungrebe has to be certain that his babies are secure – a bit like a parent checking that their child's safety belt is on before driving away in the car. The sungrebe father cannot easily see whether his chicks are safely tucked into each of the pouches, but he can feel if they are secure and deep inside the pouch. As soon as he is convinced that everyone is safe, there's no further delay.

Ready for take-off!

The Zigzag Bird

Southern Subantarctic Oceans

Out in the open ocean, the horizons seem very far away. From the safety of a large boat, sailors watch the sea surge up and then sink back down again. Grey waves tower, and then curl and crash. Behind the boat, gliding effortlessly on stiff wings and safe from the crashing waves, is an extraordinary seabird – the wandering albatross.

Albatrosses live long lives, often surviving for as many as sixty years. Every two years, a female albatross will lay just one egg. The parents take it in turns to sit on the egg for three weeks at a time, waiting patiently for their baby to hatch.

Extremely hungry, the off-duty albatross must set out across the ocean in search of a meal. Its main diet is squid, but finding enough to eat means flying over thousands of miles of water.

Being an albatross is hard work.

In the vast ocean, squid are tiny and difficult to see. If the wandering albatross wants to fill its belly, it will have to use its nose. The bird has two tiny nostrils on top of its beak. Inside these nostrils is the albatross's nose. The squid smell, and tiny particles of squid-scent float in the air, blown by the wind across the waves like an invisible plume of smoke wafting across the sea.

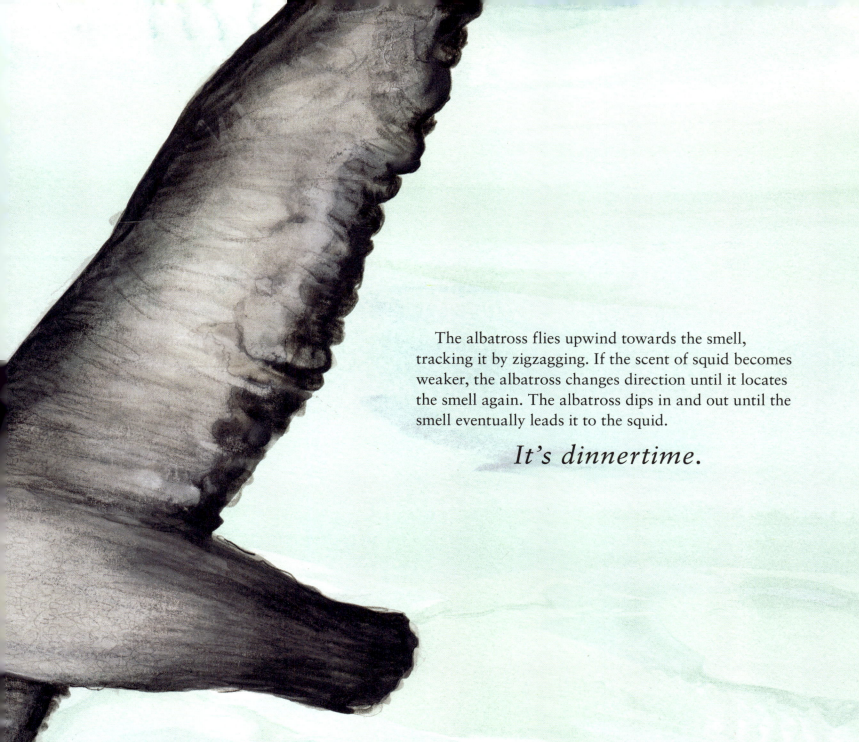

The albatross flies upwind towards the smell, tracking it by zigzagging. If the scent of squid becomes weaker, the albatross changes direction until it locates the smell again. The albatross dips in and out until the smell eventually leads it to the squid.

It's dinnertime.

The wandering albatross was given its name because of the enormous distances it covers in search of food. The bird rarely flies in a straight line. It follows a zigzag path over the sea, wing tips occasionally dipping to touch the waves.

Friends with Feathers

Central and South America, and Africa

The macaw parrot inches along its perch, chest of gold and wings of blue and eyes as bright as buttons. It bobs its head up and down, beak ajar as it waits to catch someone's eye.

'Hello? Hello? Hello-hello-hello!'

Depending on where you live, you probably have a local accent. If you move to a new part of the country, especially as a child, you may start to speak in the same accent as your new friends and playmates. Doing this makes you fit in.

Wild parrots do it too with their squawks and screeches. Like us, parrots are social creatures – they live in flocks and they often pair up for life. These are long-term friendships – parrots can live for forty years – and in the wild, pairs of parrots do everything together.

Pet parrots form a close bond with their owner. This special friendship is the same that a wild parrot would have with its mate. Many pet parrots can also copy human speech. They use their big brain and large tongue to mimic our words and catchphrases in an attempt to help them try and fit in. Talking is the parrot's way of adopting the local accent and becoming part of the group.

Parrots are clever because they can copy and remember lots of human words. Sometimes the birds even seem to say them at the right time, like squawking 'hello' when someone walks into a room, and 'cheerio' when they leave.

Does the parrot really understand what 'hello' means? Probably not … They may just learn that their owner likes to hear it. Even so, a wild parrot and its mate, or a pet parrot and its owner, can become the best of friends.

Wild parrots are usually
found in tropical rainforests.
They remarkably use their
bill as a third foot to help
them climb up trees.

35

Many birds migrate between
their summer breeding grounds
in Britain and their winter homes
in southern Europe or Africa.

The Magic Compass

Summers in Europe, winters in Africa

The robin redbreast stands to attention on an upturned spade, his little chest puffed out. The winds of change are blowing – he can feel it in the autumn breeze and see it in the piles of golden leaves strewn across the grass.

The robin surveys his home, and chirps a merry tune.

'Goodbye garden, I'll come back and see you soon!'

For now it is autumn, and there are not enough insects in Britain to feed all the robins over winter. Instead, some robins must make their way south - to Africa - where food is less scarce.

Just as a car setting out on a long journey needs a full tank of fuel, so too do small birds. Flying takes a lot of energy and, before setting off, the little robin must eat a lot of extra food and turn it into fat. This is the fuel that will carry it to its wintering grounds.

But how do little birds find their way?

Inside the robin's brain there is a 'programme' that tells it when to start eating extra food, and later, once it has a layer of fat beneath its skin, when to set off on migration. That same programme also tells it how many days it should fly for, and in what direction.

But the direction alone is not enough. Robins need to know exactly where they are on the map, but they can only do this in the dark.

Robins can detect the Earth's magnetic field – a force that determines north, south, east and west. This astonishing skill is carried out using only the robin's right eye. The eye acts like a mini-compass, showing the bird which direction to fly (south for the winter or north for the summer) even when no other landmarks are visible to guide the way.

Noisy Seabird City

Northern Hemisphere

The colony is teeming with life. High above a turbulent sea, the cliff edges are lined with hundreds of noisy residents, jostling for space. With a loud flapping of wings, the guillemot tucks itself in beside its mate, without a downward glance at the sheer rock face that tumbles down towards the sea below.

The male gently nibbles and preens the female's neck feathers. Nearby, a neighbour screeches a cheerful hello. The female squawks back. As long as the guillemot gang are together, these birds are quite content.

Preening is how guillemots keep their feathers clean. Birds usually preen themselves, but sometimes they also preen their partner. This is called allo-preening. It helps to keep a partner's plumage in tiptop condition, especially since most allo-preening is to the head and neck, parts of the body a bird cannot reach with its own beak.

For guillemots, allo-preening is less about cleanliness and more about friendship – just as it is with monkeys and apes. Partners preen each other simply because being preened feels good and they like being nice to each other. A bit like how we enjoy a hug from someone we love.

Guillemots are big fans of allo-preening. Every year, they return to the same tiny area of cliff to pair up with their partner again. Let the preening begin! Not only do guillemots carefully preen their partners, they also preen their neighbours. Because the guillemots always return to the same area, they know neighbouring pairs very well. Pairs of bird support each other, like friends, and are known for helping to protect each other's eggs from angry gulls.

These friendships can last a lifetime.

For most birds – and for all humans – the
tongue starts in the bottom of the mouth. But
the woodpecker's extra-long tongue starts just
above its eyes, looping round behind the skull
before it goes down into the mouth.

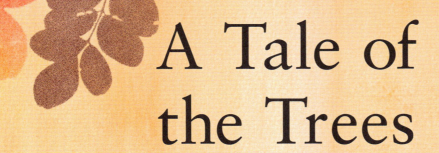

A Tale of the Trees

Europe and North America

Tap! Tap! Tap! The woodpecker shuffles up the tree trunk, tipping its head to one side. The forest is cool and earthy beneath the canopy of green. The woodpecker bounces along an ancient, twisted branch, then taps again.

TAP! TAP! TAP! TAP! TAP!

'This is my tree,' it drums out firmly. 'Kindly stay away!'

It's not hard to see how the woodpecker got its name, being a bird that finds food, creates a nesting site and talks to others – all by pecking on wood. The woodpecker's skull is incredibly tough to withstand all of that hammering, but this beautiful bird also has a sensitive side …

Woodpeckers eat insect grubs. Their favourites are the type that feed on rotting wood. To get at these grubs – the larvae of beetles – the woodpecker has to break open branches with its strong beak.

But the grubs do not want to be eaten … Hearing the woodpecker, they quickly back up the burrow and retreat inside the branch they're living in. However, the woodpecker is not deterred for it has an ingenious way of capturing grubs.

Imagine putting your hand into a long, dark tunnel and trying to sense something soft and juicy, like a peach, at the end. You cannot see the peach, nor smell it. Instead you rely on your fingertips to tell when you have found the fruit. Luckily for us, our fingertips are super-sensitive. The woodpecker's tongue works the same way and before long the grubs turn into a tasty meal.

A woodpecker's tongue is super-sticky too. The tongue easily fixes onto the grub and then drags it out of the hole to eat.

The Secret Hedgerow House

Europe and Asia

The long-tailed tit is a tiny bird, weighing little more than a teaspoonful of sugar. It has a round body and a long tail.

A flash of pink, black and white flutters
across the field. Quick as a flash, the bird darts
into the brambles and disappears from sight.
Inside the hedgerow is its own secret world.

The long-tailed tit skips and bounces through the maze of thorns and branches, towards a dome of silvery-green. Another bird pops its head out of the dome entrance, then dives back in again. The tit follows it inside where ten tiny chicks are waiting, mouths open wide.

'Feed us!'

During the autumn and winter, the long-tailed tit lives in small flocks that feed in the day and huddle together to keep warm at night. In the spring, once breeding starts, some of the birds do something astonishing – they help to raise each other's children.

The long-tailed tit's nest is beautiful. It is shaped like an egg, with an enclosed roof and an entrance hole on one side. The outside of the nest is made of moss held together with spiders' silk and then covered in lichens. Inside, the nest is lined with hundreds of feathers to help keep the parents, eggs and chicks warm.

Although the nests are camouflaged, many are destroyed by predatory birds, like crows or jays. When a pair of long-tailed tits lose their nest in this way they either start building again, or, if it is late in the breeding season, they become helpers at somebody else's.

Helping at a relative's nest is better than giving up altogether.
The more helpers there are, the more food each chick will receive.
These long-tailed tits may have failed to produce any of their
own babies, but, by helping their relatives, they have
made the best of the breeding season.

The Moth Trap

Summers in Europe and Asia, winters in Africa

The nightjar flies up into the sky. Its eyes are huge and dark, excellent for seeing in the dusky evening light. The bird swoops on silent wings across its heathland home.

A large, pale moth flutters up from the heather. The nightjar sees it at once. The bird swerves towards the moth on long, elegant wings with its mouth open wide.

SNAP!

The nightjar flies at night. During the day it sleeps on the ground or nestled into the crook of a branch. Its tawny, patterned feathers hide it perfectly from view. When it is resting, the nightjar looks just like a log. The nightjar's beak is tiny, but its mouth is huge. It is pink on the inside, and along the top part of the beak is lined with whiskery feathers. The nightjar's whiskers can pick up the slightest feelings.

A moth only has to brush the nightjar's whiskers during the chase for the bird to sense that its victim is near. The nightjar opens its beak at once, trapping the moth in its beak. This all happens so fast it is difficult to see, especially since it is dark.

The nightjar swallows down its supper, then sets off again, hungry for more.

As darkness falls the nightjar wakes, lifts its head and starts to call. The nightjar's cry is unlike that of any other bird. Imagine the sound of a lawnmower humming in the distance.

Bird Sense

Like us, birds rely on their senses.

Sight

Predatory birds, like eagles and falcons have large eyes that allow them to spot things much further away than we can. Those that fly after dark, such as nightjars and owls, can pick out shapes in poor light that no person would be able to see.

Sound

Similar types of sounds are picked up by both birds and people. Some people cannot hear the very high, whispery song of the goldcrest, but we can all hear the deep booming call of the bittern.

Birds that live in the dark, like owls or oilbirds, have much better hearing and eyesight than us. In pitch darkness, an owl can tell exactly where a mouse or lemming is, just from hearing its tiny footsteps or the rustle of leaves made by its tail.

Touch

All birds have a fine sense of touch. Birds know whether they are sitting on their eggs in the right way, when they are holding onto a branch tightly enough not to fall off, and if any of their feathers are out of place – if they are, the bird will use its beak to preen them back into position.

Taste

To us, sugar tastes sweet and salt tastes salty. We are very good at recognising lots of other tastes too. Our tongues are lined with taste buds that can pick out different types of food. Birds have taste buds too. Whereas our taste buds are along our tongues, birds' are tucked inside their mouth.

Special senses

There are other special 'senses' used by birds that we do not have and don't yet know enough about to fully understand.

Migration

Some birds have an urge to migrate — to fly a long way in a certain direction at a certain time of year. There is no migration sense organ, at least not one that we can see. The map and the programme that make a bird migrate each year are spread throughout different parts of the bird's brain and involve lots of different senses.

Weather

Some birds can sense when and where it has rained, even from a great distance. Flamingos spend their winters on the coast of Africa, but their breeding grounds lie far away inland. Flamingos can only breed when it rains enough to create large lakes full of food. The flamingos may wait at the coast for weeks until one day they suddenly fly inland, finding a rain-filled lake that is the perfect spot for them to feed and breed. How did the flamingos know it had rained?

We don't know exactly how these special senses work. But, it is what we do not know that makes birds interesting. It is what makes us want to learn more.

One day we might truly discover what it is like to be a bird.

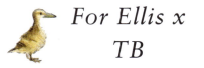

For Ellis x
TB

For Lucy, Charlotte and Max, with love x
CR

About the Author

An internationally-renowned ornithologist, **Tim Birkhead** is a Fellow of the Royal Society and Emeritus Professor of Zoology at the University of Sheffield. He has won awards for his inspirational teaching and for his many brilliant books for adults, including the bestselling *The Wisdom of Birds* and *Bird Sense*. Tim is also the recipient of the Zoological Society of London's Award for Communicating Zoology (2016), and the Society for the Study of Evolution's Stephen Jay Gould Award (2018). *What it's Like to be a Bird* is his first book for children.

About the Illustrator

Award-winning author and illustrator **Catherine Rayner** grew up in the countryside of West Yorkshire, but studied illustration at Edinburgh College of Art. She has drawn animals ever since she could hold a pencil, and they are at the centre of almost all of her children's books. Catherine has been nominated, shortlisted and longlisted for numerous awards, many of which she has won. Her awards include the BookTrust Best New Illustrator Award for Early Years for her first picture book *Augustus and His Smile* (2006), and the CILIP Kate Greenaway Medal for *Harris Finds His Feet* (2009). *What it's Like to be a Bird* is her first book for Bloomsbury.

BLOOMSBURY CHILDREN'S BOOKS
Bloomsbury Publishing Plc
50 Bedford Square, London, WC1B 3DP, UK
29 Earlsfort Terrace, Dublin 2

BLOOMSBURY, BLOOMSBURY CHILDREN'S BOOKS
and the Diana logo are trademarks of Bloomsbury Publishing Plc
First published in Great Britain 2021 by Bloomsbury Publishing Plc
Text copyright © Tim Birkhead, 2021
Illustrations copyright © Catherine Rayner, 2021

A catalogue record for this book is available from the British Library
ISBN: 9781526604125
2 4 6 8 10 9 7 5 3 1

With edits and contributions from Mandy Archer
Printed and bound in China by Leo Paper Products, Heshan, Guangdong

FSC
www.fsc.org
MIX
Paper from
responsible sources
FSC® C020056

To find out more about our authors and books visit www.bloomsbury.com
and sign up for our newsletters